Presented to

_____

_____

_____

_____

_____

For Aunt Audrey. Because of her dedication to prayer, our lives have been forever changed. We'll see you in heaven.

"For this reason I kneel before the Father, from whom his whole family in heaven and on earth derives its name. I pray that out of his glorious riches he may strengthen you with power through his Spirit in your inner being, so that Christ may dwell in your hearts through faith. And I pray that you, being rooted and established in love, may have power, together with all the saints, to grasp how wide and long and high and deep is the love of Christ, and to know this love that surpasses knowledge—that you may be filled to the measure of all the fullness of God."

-Ephesians 3:14-19

In memory of...

_____

_____

_____

_____

*W*ent to heaven on...

_____

_____

_____

_____

WinePress Publishing (PO Box 428, Enumclaw, WA 98022) functions only as book publisher. As such, the ultimate design and layout are by Jessica Caskey, some photography by Julie Fannin, content, editorial accuracy, and views expressed or implied in this work are those of the author.

ISBN 13: 978-1-57921-891-1
ISBN 10: 1-57921-891-1
Library of Congress Catalog Card Number: 2006940840

Printed in Colombia.

To my husband, Daryl, a man of great faith. You supported me when *I'll See You In Heaven* was just a dream. I love you.

Vickie

To my mother, you have never ceased to believe great things for me. I love you.

Jaime

I'll see you in Heaven

Vickie Funston & Jaime Broxson

WINEPRESS WP PUBLISHING

Foreword

The loss of a loved one is a reality that every person will eventually have to face. Though it may be inevitable, it is always difficult, and most times unexpected. If you have experienced loss, this book was written with the intention of communicating God's heart for you.

God's hand has been on this project since the very beginning. The process began in 2001 when I received a prophetic word that I was to write a book for the Lord. Three years later I had a dream. It was this book. I recorded the concept and tucked it away while prayerfully pondering how it might come about. It was two more years before the Lord answered my prayers and started showing me His plan for *I'll See You In Heaven.*

In the fall of 2006, while my niece, Jaime, was attending Bible college, she received a similar prophetic word. The word that Jaime was a writer resonated in my heart as I considered this book. Suddenly I began to see God's plan unfolding before my eyes and how Jaime was going to be a part of it. It was quite evident that the Lord had orchestrated these events—that His desire was for us to seek His heart in writing this book together.

Jaime and I strongly believe that the words in this book are straight from the heart of God. The Lord is personal and wants to provide comfort and encouragement in your time of grief. In a world where time is taken for granted and loss can come suddenly, our hope is that He will help you find strength through this book as you hear the voice of your lost loved one saying, "I'll see you in heaven."

- Vickie

"*Precious in the sight of the Lord is the death of those faithful to Him.*"

-Psalm 116:15

Death always comes too soon. It seems like no matter how many days God gives us on earth, our time is too short. As we look back on our lives, we dream of all the things we might have done—all the adventures and joys we could have experienced if only we had more time—if only we had an eternity.

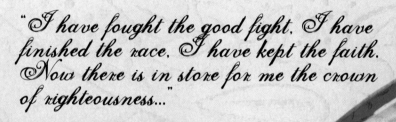

"I have fought the good fight, I have finished the race, I have kept the faith. Now there is in store for me the crown of righteousness..."

-2 Timothy 4:7-8

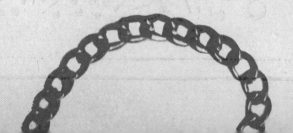

Standing on the other side of death, I now understand the reality of eternity. Eternity begins the day we are born. The gifts God gives us begin on that day. They do not end when we die; they carry on. We enjoy some of the gifts on earth's side of eternity; others must wait for heaven's side.

When I leave my home on earth, I enter my heavenly residence. I bring with me memories of life and love. These are the true gifts that last. Invest in eternal things that will make you rich when you arrive and join me here.

"For this world is not our permanent home; we are looking forward to a home yet to come."

-Hebrews 13:14

The Book of Life lists the names of those who choose the saving grace of Jesus. If your name is written there, as mine is, we will see each other again. It ensures my entrance into heaven, just as it will ensure yours.

"All who are victorious will be clothed in white. I will never erase their names from the Book of Life, but I will announce before my Father and his angels that they are mine."

-Revelation 3:5

As I cross the threshold into heaven, the first face I behold is that of Jesus. Love and kindness such as I have never known fill His eyes. I immediately fall at His feet, overwhelmed in His presence. He lifts my face toward His and places a glorious crown upon my head.

I am soon surrounded by the faces of loved ones and friends who have gone before me. The perfect love of Jesus and the brilliance of heaven enhance our joyful reunion.

$\mathscr{T}$he landscape of heaven combines the beauty of earth's greatest features with a supernatural twist.

$\mathscr{P}$earl gates surround the heavenly city. Precious jewels decorate the foundations of its walls. They shine with colors no eye outside of heaven has ever seen.

The streets of the heavenly city are made of gold—gold so pure you can see right through it. There is no sun; we don't need it. The light of God's presence shines as bright and as far as eternity reaches.

A mighty river flows from the throne of God, through the city. Life-giving trees line the river, and its waters are as clear as crystal.

*O*ur heavenly homes are mansions fit for royalty, and every meal is a feast. Heaven is the most beautiful place our eyes will ever behold.

*J*esus is the centerpiece of heaven. Everything I see here reflects His majesty. His glory illuminates the skies, and the sweet-smelling fragrance of His Spirit fills the air.

"And I heard the voices of thousands
and millions of angels around the throne
and they sang in a mighty chorus:
'Worthy is the Lamb to receive power
and riches and wisdom and strength
and honor and glory and blessing.'"

-Revelation 5:11, 12

$\mathcal{I}$ spend precious moments worshiping before the throne. I sing with the angels. No choir is as commanding, no melody as captivating, as that of the angelic host. When you sing of God's holiness on earth know that you are joining me and all of heaven in that song.

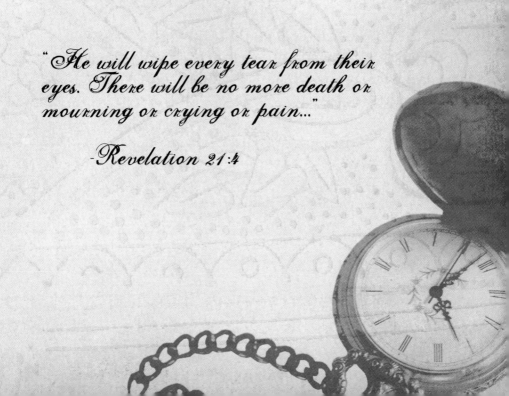

"He will wipe every tear from their eyes. There will be no more death or mourning or crying or pain..."

-Revelation 21:4

Nowhere in heaven do I find the sadness and pain that you see on earth. There is no loneliness, no rejection, no fear. I have never felt such peace.

$\mathcal{D}$eath has carried me into the life I was destined for. I am more alive now than I have ever been. No longer bound by a fallen world, I am free to be whom I was created to be. My joy is complete, my brokenness restored, and my doubt gone forever.

When you think about how much you miss me, remember this place. Remember that I am here, and that I am whole. Remember that one day we will see each other again.

I'll See You
In Heaven

Vickie's Journey

The greatest decision I have ever made was the choice to serve and accept Jesus Christ as my Savior. I was introduced to Him through missionaries that came to teach the Word of God to the neighborhood kids in my aunt and uncle's basement. I was nine years old at the time. This was the beginning of a relationship that would profoundly affect the rest of my life. The wonderful life I live today is a direct result of the choice I made that day. As I have walked the path that my Jesus set before me. I cannot say that I have always stayed on course or that I have always made the right decisions.

I cannot say that this path has not included difficult turns and unexpected struggles, but I can say that Jesus has always been the Constant in my life. I could not have gone where I've been, nor could I go where I am headed without Christ by my side. He is my Joy, my Peace, my Protector, and the Miracle that has saved me. I look forward to the day when I stand before Him and He says to me, "Well done my Daughter."

Jaime's Journey

Growing up, I never really had a chance to know my father. He was alive, but because of the circumstances surrounding my birth, I didn't enjoy the privilege of having him in my life. When I would question her, my mom would always tell me about my father in heaven. She would tell me that I had the very best Daddy in the whole wide world because God was my Daddy. He would never leave me, never disappoint me; He was a perfect Daddy and He chose me to be His little girl. I would imagine what heaven was like and I would picture myself sitting in my Daddy's lap while He orchestrated the happenings of the world.

Now, as an adult, I still relate to God as my Heavenly Father. I still picture myself wrapped in His strong arms as His plan for my life unfolds. I am who I am because of my Dad. One day, when my hope of heaven is fulfilled, I will see Him face to face—what a glorious Father-daughter reunion it will be!

Salvation

The Promise of a Home in Heaven

The promise of a home in heaven is the hope of all those who believe in Jesus Christ. Knowing that our loved ones are healed and whole in the presence of Jesus softens even the deepest of grief. Knowing that we will get to see them again someday means that joy can be found even in the saddest circumstances. If you read this book and desire to share in that hope please say this prayer:

Jesus, I acknowledge that you are the only way to heaven. Thank you for giving your life for me so that I might live for eternity with you and those that I love. I ask that you would forgive me and accept me as your own today. Be my Savior. In Jesus' name,

Amen.

Jesus Christ is the Hope of Heaven. Your decision to accept Him as your Savior is the greatest and most amazing decision you will ever make. All the angels in heaven, along with your lost loved one, are rejoicing over you and saying, "I'll See You in Heaven!"

"For God so loved the world that He gave His one and only Son, that whoever believes in Him shall not perish but have eternal life. For God did not send His son into the world to condemn the world, but to save the world through Him."

-John 3:16-17

"If you confess with your mouth...'Jesus is Lord' and believe in your heart that God raised Him from the dead, you will be saved."

-Romans 10:9

Memories of Life and Love

_____

_____

_____

_____

_____

_____

_____

_____

_____

_____